National State Auditors Association
and the
U. S. General Accounting Office

A Joint Initiative

Management Planning Guide for Information Systems Security Auditing

December 10, 2001

References to specific vendors, services, products, and Web sites noted throughout this document are included as examples of information available on information security. Such references do not constitute a recommendation or endorsement. Readers should keep in mind that the accuracy, timeliness, and value of Web site information can vary widely and should take appropriate steps to verify any Web-based information they intend to rely on.

December 10, 2001

On behalf of the U. S. General Accounting Office (GAO) and the National State Auditors Association (NSAA), it is our pleasure to present this *Management Planning Guide for Information Systems Security Auditing.*

The rapid and dramatic advances in information technology (IT) in recent years have without question generated tremendous benefits. At the same time, however, they have created significant, unprecedented risks to government operations. Computer security has, in turn, become much more important as all levels of government utilize information systems security measures to avoid data tampering, fraud, disruptions in critical operations, and inappropriate disclosure of sensitive information. Such use of computer security is essential in minimizing the risk of malicious attacks from individuals and groups.

To be effective in ensuring accountability, auditors must be able to evaluate information systems security and offer recommendations for reducing security risks to an acceptable level. To do so, they must possess the appropriate resources and skills.

This guide is intended to help audit organizations respond to this expanding use of IT and the concomitant risks that flow from such pervasive use by governments. It applies to any evaluative government organization, regardless of size or current methodology. Directed primarily at executives and senior managers, the guide covers the steps involved in establishing or enhancing an information security auditing capability: planning, developing a strategy, implementing the capability, and assessing results.

We hope this guide—a cooperative effort among those at the federal, state, and local levels—will assist governments in meeting the challenge of keeping pace with the rapid evolution and deployment of new information technology. We wish to extend sincere appreciation to the task force responsible for preparing this guide, particularly the work of task force leaders Carol Langelier of GAO and Jon Ingram of the Office of Florida Auditor General.

Additional copies of the guide are available at the Web sites of both GAO (*www.gao.gov*) and the National Association of State Auditors, Comptrollers, and Treasurers (*www.nasact.org*). For further information about the guide, please contact any of the task force members listed on the next page.

Sincerely,

David M. Walker
Comptroller General
of the United States

Ronald L. Jones
President, NSAA
Chief Examiner, Alabama

i

**National State Auditors Association
and the
U. S. General Accounting Office**

**Joint Information Systems Security Audit Initiative
Management Planning Guide Committee**

Co-Chairs

Carol Langelier
U.S. General Accounting Office
langelierc@gao.gov

Jon Ingram, FL
Office of the Auditor General
joningram@aud.state.fl.us

Members

Andy Bishop, NJ
Office of Legislative Services

Beth Breier, City of Tallahassee
Office of the City Auditor
breierb@talgov.com

Gail Chase, ME
Department of Audit
gail.chase@state.me.us

John Clinch, NH
Legislative Budget Office
john.clinch@leg.state.nh.us

Mike Cragin, LA
Office of the Legislative Auditor
mcragin@lla.state.la.us

Bob Dacey
U. S. General Accounting Office
daceyr@gao.gov

Allan Foster, KS
Legislative Division of Post Audit
allanf@lpa.state.ks.us

Darrell Heim
U. S. General Accounting Office
heimd@gao.gov

Walter Irving, NY
Office of the State Comptroller
wirving@osc.state.ny.us

Bob Koslowski, MD
Office of Legislative Audits
rkoslowski@ola.state.md.us

Beth Pendergrass, TN
Comptroller of the Treasury
Division of State Audit
bpenderg@mail.state.tn.us

Nancy Rainosek, TX
State Auditor's Office
nrainosek@sao.state.tx.us

Chuck Richardson, TN
Comptroller of the Treasury,
Division of State Audit
crichardson@mail.state.tn.us

Martin Vernon, NC
Office of the State Auditor
martin_vernon@ncauditor.net

Sharron Walker, AZ
Office of the Auditor General
swalker@auditorgen.state.az.us

Contents

Appendices

Table

I. Introduction and Background

Purpose of the guide
Background
Information systems security auditing
Information security control, assessment, and assurance
State and local government IS audit organizations
Applicable legislation
Influencing legislation
Content of this guide

Purpose of the Guide

Rapid and dramatic advances in information technology (IT), while offering tremendous benefits, have also created significant and unprecedented risks to government operations. Federal, state, and local governments depend heavily on information systems (IS) security measures to avoid data tampering, fraud, inappropriate access to and disclosure of sensitive information, and disruptions in critical operations. These risks are expected to only continue to escalate as wireless and other technologies emerge. Government auditors, to be effective instruments of accountability, need to be able to evaluate IS security and offer recommendations for reducing the security risk to an acceptably low level. Further, the growing importance of IT in performing daily operational activities, along with the elimination of paper-based evidence and audit trails, demands that auditors consider the effectiveness of IT controls during the course of financial and performance audits. To do so, auditors must acquire and maintain the appropriate resources and skill sets—a daunting challenge in an era of rapid evolution and deployment of new information technology. Likewise, government audit organizations need to take stock of their IS security audit capabilities and ensure that strategies exist for their continued development and enhancement.

This guide was prepared by members of the National State Auditors Association (NSAA) and auditors from local governments in cooperation with staff of the United States General Accounting Office (GAO). It is intended to aid government audit organizations in responding to the risks attributable to the pervasive and dynamic effects of the expanding use of information technology by governments. Also, it is intended to be pertinent to any government audit organization, regardless of its size and current methodology. Directed primarily at senior and executive audit management, the guide leads the reader through the steps for establishing or enhancing an information security auditing capability. These include planning, developing a strategy, implementing the capability, and assessing results.

Background

Electronic information is essential to the achievement of government organizational objectives. Its reliability, integrity, and availability are significant concerns in most audits. The use of computer networks, particularly the Internet, is revolutionizing the way government conducts business. While the benefits have been enormous and vast amounts of information are now literally at our fingertips, these interconnections also pose significant risks to computer systems, information, and to the critical operations and infrastructures they support. Infrastructure elements such as telecommunications, power distribution, national defense, law enforcement, and government and emergency services are subject to these risks. The same factors that benefit operations—speed and accessibility—if not properly controlled, can leave them vulnerable to fraud, sabotage, and malicious or mischievous acts. In addition, natural disasters and inadvertent errors by authorized computer users can have devastating consequences if information resources are poorly protected. Recent publicized disruptions caused by virus, worm, and denial of service attacks on both commercial and governmental Web sites illustrate the potential for damage.

Computer security is of increasing importance to all levels of government in minimizing the risk of malicious attacks from individuals and groups. These risks include the fraudulent loss or misuse of government resources, unauthorized access to release of sensitive information such as tax and medical records, disruption of critical operations through viruses or hacker attacks, and modification or destruction of data. The risk that information attacks will threaten vital national interests increases with the following developments in information technology:

- Monies are increasingly transferred electronically between and among governmental agencies, commercial enterprises, and individuals.

- Governments are rapidly expanding their use of electronic commerce.

- National defense and intelligence communities increasingly rely on commercially available information technology.

- Public utilities and telecommunications increasingly rely on computer systems to manage everyday operations.

- More and more sensitive economic and commercial information is exchanged electronically.

- Computer systems are rapidly increasing in complexity and interconnectivity.

- Easy-to-use hacker tools are readily available, and hacker activity is increasing.

- Paper supporting documents are being reduced or eliminated.

Each of these factors significantly increases the need for ensuring the privacy, security, and availability of state and local government systems.

Although as many as 80 percent of security breaches are probably never reported, the number of reported incidents is growing dramatically. For example, the number of incidents handled by Carnegie-Mellon University's CERT Coordination Center[1] has multiplied over 86 times since 1990,[2] rising from 252 in 1990 to 21,756 in 2000. Further, the Center has handled over 34,000 incidents during the first three quarters of 2001. Similarly, the Federal Bureau of Investigation (FBI) reports that its case load of computer intrusion-related cases is more than doubling every year. The fifth annual survey conducted by the Computer Security Institute in cooperation with the FBI found that 70 percent of respondents (primarily large corporations and government agencies) had detected serious computer security breaches within the last 12 months and that quantifiable financial losses had increased over past years.[3]

Are agencies responding to the call for greater security? There is great cause for concern regarding this question, since GAO's November 2001 analyses[4] of computer security identified significant weaknesses in each of the 24 major agencies covered by its reviews. The weaknesses identified place a broad array of federal operations and assets at risk of fraud, misuse, and disruption. For example, weaknesses at the Department of Treasury increase the risk of fraud associated with billions of dollars of federal payments and collections, and weaknesses at the Department of Defense increase the vulnerability of various military operations that support the department's war-fighting capability. Further, information security weaknesses place enormous amounts of confidential data, ranging from personal, financial, tax, and health data to proprietary business information, at risk of inappropriate disclosure.

Reviews of general and application controls often point up basic control weaknesses in IT systems of state agencies as well. Typical weaknesses include the following:

- Lack of formal IT planning mechanisms with the result that IT does not serve the agency's pressing needs or does not do so in a timely and secure manner;

---

[1]Originally called the Computer Emergency Response Team, the center was established in 1988 by the Defense Advanced Research Projects Agency. It is charged with (1) establishing a capability to quickly and effectively coordinate communication among experts in order to limit the damage associated with, and respond to, incidents and (2) building awareness of security issues across the Internet community.

[2] Source: CERT Coordination Center Statistics, 1988–2001 (www.cert.org/stats/cert_stats html).

[3]*Issues and Trends: 2000 CSI/FBI Computer Crime and Security Survey* (The Computer Security Institute, March 2000).

[4] *Computer Security: Improvements Needed to Reduce Risks to Critical Federal Operations and Assets* (GAO-02-231T, November 9, 2001).

- Lack of formal security policies resulting in a piecemeal or "after-an-incident" approach to security;

- Inadequate program change control leaving software vulnerable to unauthorized changes;

- Little or no awareness of key security issues and inadequate technical staff to address the issues;

- Failure to take full advantage of all security software features such as selective monitoring capabilities, enforcement of stringent password rules, and review of key security reports.

- Inadequate user involvement in testing and sign-off for new applications resulting in systems that fail to meet user functional requirements or confidentiality, integrity, and availability needs.

- Installation of software or upgrades without adequate attention to the default configurations or default passwords.

- Virus definitions that are not kept up-to-date.

- Inadequate continuity of operation plans.

- Failure to formally assign security administration responsibilities to staff who are technically competent, independent, and report to senior management.

Also of concern is a relatively recent threat. A number of state agencies' Web sites were hacked through a vulnerability in a widely used vendor's operating system. The time between the discovery of the vulnerability by the vendor and the notification to users that a special software patch should be applied was a matter of days. The need for immediate notification of vulnerabilities and a subsequent need to react immediately will mean higher standards for security/network administration groups who may have limited staff and technical knowledge.

Similarly, a review of local government audit abstracts published in the *National Association of Local Government Auditors Journal* shows a number of common problems related to information security, including lack of user awareness, unnecessarily high access rights, and lack of segregation of duties, among others.

Most vulnerabilities identified in the GAO reports and elsewhere resulted from the lack of fundamental computer security controls: information security management program, physical and logical access controls, software change controls, segregated duties, and continuity of operations. These results reinforce the need for the audit community to be concerned with the management of security and implementation of information security controls.

The assessment of security controls over certain financial and program documents has always been an important part of an audit. This objective has not been changed by the growing use of networks, including the Internet, for delivery of government services. However, this development does give rise to the need for an audit team to look for different controls and to include IS security as a part of the risk assessment and audit process.

Information Systems Security Auditing

IS security auditing involves providing independent evaluations of an organization's policies, procedures, standards, measures, and practices for safeguarding electronic information from loss, damage, unintended disclosure, or denial of availability. The broadest scope of work includes the assessment of general and application controls. The current state of technology requires audit steps that relate to testing controls of access paths resulting from the connectivity of local-area networks, wide-area networks, intranet, Internet, etc., in the IT environment.

The results of these evaluations are generally directed to the organization's management, legislative bodies, other auditors, or the public. IS security auditing may be performed in engagements where

- the specific audit objective is to evaluate security, or

- the audit objectives are much broader, but evaluating security is a necessary subset. (For example, an audit objective such as financial statement assurance or program evaluation frequently may be met only when there is assurance that the security of the financial or program data is adequate.)

Information Security Control, Assessment, and Assurance

Professional audit organizations have recognized the need for increased assurances regarding critical data and are increasingly emphasizing and providing guidance on IS security auditing. For example:

- The Information Systems Audit and Control Association (ISACA) provides detailed guidance and technical resources relating to audit and control of information technology. The related Information Systems Audit and Control Foundation (ISACF) and sponsors have prepared COBIT: *Control Objectives for Information and Related Technology,* a set of IT audit guidelines. According to ISACF, "COBIT is intended to be the breakthrough IT governance tool that helps in understanding and managing the risks associated with information and related IT."

- NSAA's annual Mid-management and IT Peer Conference program has placed significant emphasis on presentation of IT security assessment as practiced by various member states.

- GAO's *Federal Information System Controls Audit Manual* (FISCAM)[5] describes the computer-related controls, including security controls, that auditors should consider when assessing the integrity, reliability, and availability of computerized data. This guide is applied by GAO and Inspectors General primarily in support of financial statement audits and is available for use by other government auditors.

- The American Institute of Certified Public Accountants (AICPA) has recognized both the need for and the opportunities associated with providing consulting and assurance services to Internet-enabled businesses and the consumer public, as well as users of traditional systems. Information security controls have been identified among the AICPA's list of annual "top technologies." With the Canadian Institute of Chartered Accountants, the AICPA has also developed WebTrust Assurance Services to provide a framework for independent verification of Web-enabled system reliability and the security of consumer information. These two organizations also jointly developed SysTrust™ Principles and Criteria for Systems Reliability, which provides a framework for assessing the reliability of systems.

Users of e-government services may expect or require similar assurances in the future.

- The GAO and AICPA, in recent changes to auditing standards, place a stronger emphasis on assessing the risk associated with information technology and evaluating relevant IT controls, including controls over information security. These changes recognize that obtaining sufficient evidence in a financial statement or performance audit now frequently requires consideration of IT controls over data reliability. Examples of auditing standards revisions that place a stronger emphasis on IT can be found in appendix A.

Clearly, the audit profession continues to adapt and evolve in response to the needs for assurance of information security both in existing traditional information systems and in emerging Internet-enabled services.

State and Local Government IS Audit Organizations

The size of the audit organization and the placement of the IS audit function within the organization may affect strategies for establishing an IS security audit capability. State and local government audit organizations vary widely in both the size and the organization of their IS audit functions. Some audit agencies have not established an IS audit function at all, and instead contract for those services. Others integrate their IS auditors into their financial or operational audit teams. Still others have separate IS audit groups who work in support of the financial or operational teams. Despite these variations, however, audit organizations should be able to establish an IS security audit capability in a manner appropriate for the audit organization's size, structure, and mission.

Applicable Legislation

Since 1974, a series of federal laws, rules, and directives have addressed information security (see list in appendix B). These federal requirements apply not only to federal agencies, but also to organizations that process information for federal purposes, including all state and local agencies receiving federal funding. In addition to federal

---

[5] *Federal Information System Controls Audit Manual* (GAO/AIMD-12.19.6, January 1999).

laws and regulations, most states have passed computer crime or fraud and abuse laws that provide protections for individuals and corporations.

The 107th Congress is considering more laws on computer crime. For example, HR 1017, the Anti-Spamming Act of 2001, would prohibit the unsolicited e-mail known as "spam." HR 347, the Consumer Online Privacy and Disclosure Act, would require the Federal Trade Commission to prescribe regulations to protect the privacy of personal information collected from and about individuals on the Internet, to provide greater individual control over the collection and use of that information, and for other purposes.

Influencing Legislation

Government auditors are in a unique position to promote and encourage a concerted response to the expanding information security risks facing today's public sector. A critical aspect of this is raising awareness among legislators of the risks to information technology. Without a clear recognition of the seriousness of information security risks, legislators may not provide sufficient funding of information security initiatives to facilitate an effective response to these risks. Raising awareness could be done through several means, such as legislative briefings, speeches, and high-level security assessments. Some states have hired contractors to perform network vulnerability testing to demonstrate government exposure to common, known vulnerabilities.

Audit organizations supported by legislative appropriations may need to convince their legislators of the importance of funding the information system security capability, which may be costly to develop and maintain. These organizations need to be prepared to state a convincing case to legislators of the importance of information systems security. After audit management has prepared an IS security audit strategic plan and has identified associated costs, a plan to approach the legislature for funding may need to be drafted. Often organizations find funding to be an ongoing challenge. In the current economic climate, full funding may not be readily available. Interim adjustments may thus be needed for both the approach to the legislature and the audit strategy.

Content of This Guide

This guide provides specific information intended to assist in planning and developing strategies for developing or enhancing the IS security audit capability, applying the capability on specific engagements, and measuring and monitoring the performance of the IS security audit activities. The first section, on developing a strategic plan, covers developing a mission statement and objectives for the IS security audit capability, assessing IS security audit readiness, devising criteria for project selection, and linking objectives to the supporting activities. The second section, on measuring and monitoring the audit capability once it is established, covers purpose, monitoring processes, benchmarking, and performance and reporting measures. Appendices provide supplementary information, including a discussion of auditing standards and IT controls, applicable legislation, an assessment tool, a self-assessment questionnaire for IS security audit personnel, an IT security curriculum, Web sites providing training information, and other Web resources.

II. Developing a Strategic Plan for an IS Security Auditing Capability

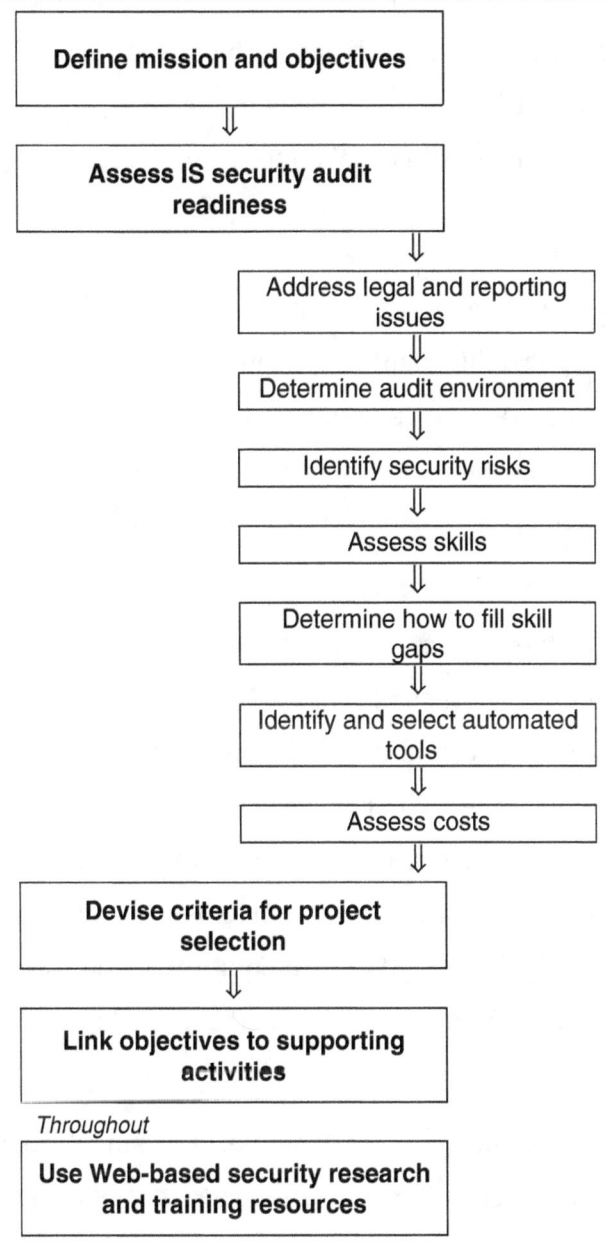

Define mission and objectives

⇓

Assess IS security audit readiness

⇓

Address legal and reporting issues

⇓

Determine audit environment

⇓

Identify security risks

⇓

Assess skills

⇓

Determine how to fill skill gaps

⇓

Identify and select automated tools

⇓

Assess costs

⇓

Devise criteria for project selection

⇓

Link objectives to supporting activities

Throughout

Use Web-based security research and training resources

As shown in the figure above, organizations should follow several steps to plan to formulate or enhance an IS security audit capability. First, the organization needs to define the mission and objectives of such a capability. Next, the organization should assess its own IS security audit readiness. This assessment requires that a range of issues be considered: legal issues, reporting constraints, the audit environment, security vulnerabilities, skills, automated tools, and costs. Organizations must also plan how to choose what IS security audit projects should be done: both stand-alone IS security audit projects and those projects requiring support from the IS security audit capability. When the planning is completed, organizations should link the objectives chosen in the first step to the activities required to support them. Throughout the process, organizations should not neglect the resources available on the Web for research and training.

Define Mission and Objectives

A mission statement for the IS security audit capability should be established. This document should outline the responsibility, authority, and accountability of the IS security audit capability. In addition, a vision statement and a statement of values and goals should be created. These statements serve to further define the mission of the IS security audit capability and set the stage to define the specific objectives desired by agency management.

Deciding on your organization's objectives for creating or enhancing an IS security audit capability will aid you in identifying the types of tools, skills, and training needed. Objectives should be defined beforehand, without first considering how and by whom the objectives would be met (for example, whether resources would be in-house, contractor, shared staff, or some combination). Also, consider focusing on a three- to five-year planning horizon rather than on what can be implemented immediately. Setting interim milestones will help to achieve a staged implementation of your planned strategy. Among the many potential objectives for an IS security audit capability, several types are common:

- To support financial statement audits by, for example, assessing IS security controls. This assessment may affect the nature and extent of financial audit steps to be performed, as well as provide timely support for needed improvements in computer-related controls.[6]

- To support performance audits, such as assessing how well an information system protects the integrity and reliability of data and the effect of this level of protection on program performance.

- To supplement IT audits by assessing the effectiveness of security within the context of a general and/or application-specific controls audit.

- To provide independent system security audits, so that risks are clearly identified and can be addressed.

- To support investigative and /or forensic audits, for example by identifying unauthorized access to and manipulation of sensitive data.

- To provide support for sophisticated data analysis and extraction through computer-assisted audit techniques (CAATs).

- To provide an auditor's perspective on IS security during system development, so that controls can be appropriately designed into the system.

Your organization's objectives for developing an IS audit capability may combine the above or vary from them. Whatever the objectives, identifying them beforehand will provide a sound cornerstone on which to build the capability.

Assess IS Security Audit Readiness

In building an IS security audit capability, management should assess the organization's IS security audit readiness by taking into account the relevant factors discussed below. Establishing a baseline in these areas by identifying strengths and weaknesses will help an organization determine the best way to proceed. In many instances, this process will determine what is practical to implement within given time and budget constraints.

---

[6] The recent AICPA Statement on Auditing Standards (SAS) No. 94, *The Effect of Information Technology on the Auditor's Assessment of Internal Control in a Financial Statement Audit,* provides relevant guidance.

Address Legal and Reporting Issues

In developing an information security audit capability and in performing security audits, legal and reporting issues may arise of which an organization needs to be aware. You should consult with your legal counsel before establishing or extending the security audit capability so that legal barriers can be identified and resolved. Potential legal and reporting issues include the following:

- Your organization's right to review IS security issues.

- State laws regarding unauthorized access to sensitive data or "hacker" type activity. Analyze your state laws pertaining to computer crimes—particularly those relevant to penetration testing—to determine how the IS security audit capability can operate effectively within those bounds.

- Potential liability issues. Liability concerns may arise if penetration testing inadvertently causes problems with a critical system. While the risk of this happening may be low, steps should be taken to limit such exposure.

- Security clearances or background checks. If these are required, this issue is especially critical for a security audit capability that uses consultants or other third parties. Your state or agency may also have personnel policies governing your ability to perform background checks or security clearances. Further, performing such checks may involve costs. Also, your audit organization or state may want to obtain security clearances to obtain additional assurances concerning those staff who have access to sensitive system information.

- Provisions of the public records law. Potential issues include both restrictions and excessively permissive requirements. For example, there may be prohibitions against reporting security information—or the reverse: you might be required to provide access upon request to working papers containing sensitive, detailed security information.

Even if no public records laws apply, you should assess the level of detail included in your reports. If your organization posts audit reports on the Internet, the information is accessible to virtually anyone, anywhere. Posting detailed security findings may expose an information system to more risk than if no audit had been performed.

Once potential barriers have been identified, you can determine feasible solutions. As one example, GAO and some states use separate confidential or "Limited Official Use" (LOU) reports to detail IS security issues. The publicly issued report addresses security issues in more general terms and gives only general recommendations.

If potential barriers are identified during this assessment, the next step is to determine whether the environment can be changed or if the barrier prevents your organization from effectively forming an IS security audit capability.

Determine Audit Environment

Along with experienced personnel to perform security audits, an IS security audit capability must have relevant tools, techniques, and practice aids available to assist the auditors with their audit tasks. Decisions on obtaining such tools, techniques, and practice aids, along with the appropriate expertise to use them, must be based on the hardware, system software, and applications that constitute the audit environment. With systems becoming more and more interconnected, the hardware and software that make up and connect these systems are critical. In addition, the technical components that provide network, Internet, and intranet connectivity must be identified. An audit organization should develop an inventory of this infrastructure, which should be periodically refreshed since computer systems are extremely fluid, and projections are that technology will continue to advance rapidly.

In addition, it is important to keep informed on emerging technologies and related control issues. These new technologies may soon be integrated into your audit environment, and auditing them may require additional expertise and automated tools.

Appendix C provides a questionnaire that can assist you in collecting the type of IS infrastructure information needed to understand your audit environment. Sources of this information may include any prior audit history and other studies performed by outside contractors. Depending on the size of your audit environment, you may not be able to readily determine exact counts of the various hardware and software components. For this purpose, an estimate of the number of systems involved will suffice. Also, the questionnaire can be completed by agency personnel.

Identify Security Risks

The information security risks confronting an organization will vary with the nature of the processing performed by the organization and the sensitivity of the information processed. To fully consider these risks, the auditor should develop comprehensive information concerning the organization's computer operations and significant applications.[7] This information should be documented and generally will include

- the significance and nature of the programs and functions, such as public protection and safety, supported by automated systems;

- the sensitivity or confidentiality of the information processed;

- the types of computer processing performed (standalone, distributed, or networked);

- the specific hardware and software constituting the computer configuration, including (1) the type, number, and location of primary central processing units and peripherals, (2) the role of microcomputers, and (3) how such units are interconnected;

- the nature of software utilities used at computer processing locations that provide the ability to add, alter, or delete information stored in data files, databases, and program libraries;

- the nature of software used to restrict access to programs and data at computer processing locations;

- significant computerized communications networks (including firewalls and network control devices), interfaces to other computer systems and the Internet, and the ability to upload and/or download information;

- significant changes since any prior audits/reviews;

- the general types and extent of significant purchased software used;

- the general types and extent of significant software developed in-house;

---

[7] The audited entity is generally responsible for the completion of a security risk assessment which the auditor should obtain and build upon.

- how (interactive or noninteractive) and where data are entered and reported;

- the approximate number of transactions and related monetary amounts processed by each significant system;

- the organization and staffing at the organization's data processing and software development sites, including recent key staff and organizational changes;

- the organization's reliance on service bureaus or other agencies for computer processing support;

- results of past internal and external reviews, including those conducted by inspector general staff and consultants specializing in security matters; and

- compliance with relevant legal and regulatory requirements.

The identification of security risks has a direct relationship to the audit environment assessed in the preceding section. An organization's hardware/software infrastructure and the extent and type of computer interconnectivity used by the organization all have a bearing on the types of security risks confronting the organization. Further, the infrastructure and interconnectivity will dictate the skills and tools needed by the auditor to efficiently and effectively assess the adequacy of these security risks. Any one auditor should not be expected to have all the skills or abilities necessary to perform each of the tasks to successfully complete an information security audit. However, the audit team collectively should possess the requisite skills.

Assess Skills

A key component of planning to create or upgrade a successful IS security audit capability includes determining the current staff's knowledge, skills, and abilities to determine what the audit capability is now and what expertise must be acquired. Any expertise gap can be filled through hiring, training, contracting, or staff sharing.

Recently the U.S. General Accounting Office and the National State Auditors Association collaborated to develop a questionnaire to assist in the assessment of existing capabilities in the various state audit offices. The survey asks individuals to rate their own capabilities to assess or evaluate various technology areas or environments. Most respondents rated their capability in most categories of technology at the lowest level:

capable versus *expert* or *proficient*. Further, in most categories, a significant percentage of respondents reported a desire for training/experience. For example, out of 75 categories, 55 had greater than 40 percent of the respondents wanting more training or experience, while in 31 categories, more than 50 percent of respondents expressed this desire. The survey, conducted in the spring of 2001, reflects 134 respondents from 24 state offices.

This questionnaire, included in appendix D, can help in assessing the IS security audit skills of the current staff. The electronic format makes completing this assessment and summarizing the results less formidable. An organization can then determine how to proceed in building its capacity for IS security audits.

Generally accepted government auditing standards (GAGAS) state that the "staff assigned to conduct the audit should collectively possess adequate professional proficiency for the tasks required." The standards further require that if the work involves a review of computerized systems, the team should include persons with computer audit skills.[8] These skills are often described in terms of *knowledge, skills, and abilities* (KSAs). KSAs are typically used in job position descriptions and job announcements to describe the attributes required for holders of particular jobs. These terms are defined as follows:

Knowledge—the foundation upon which skills and abilities are built. Knowledge is an organized body of information, facts, principles, or procedures that, if applied, makes adequate performance of a job possible. An example is knowledge of tools and techniques used to establish logical access control over an information system.

Skill—the proficient manual, verbal, or mental manipulation of people, ideas, or things. A skill is demonstrable and implies a degree of proficiency. For example, a person may be skilled in operating a personal computer to prepare electronic spreadsheets or in using a software product to conduct an automated review of the integrity of an operating system.

Ability—the power to perform a job function while applying or using the essential knowledge. Abilities are evidenced through activities or behaviors required to do a job. An example is the ability to apply knowledge about logical access controls to evaluate the adequacy of an organization's implementation of such controls.

A staff member's knowledge, skills, and abilities can be categorized in accordance with FISCAM audit areas.[9] Table 1 is an overview of the knowledge, skills, and abilities that a team needs to effectively perform audit procedures in a computer-based environment. It assumes a level of proficiency in performing basic auditing tasks, such as interviewing, gathering and documenting evidence, communicating both orally and in writing, and managing projects. It focuses on attributes associated specifically with computer security auditing. Although each staff member assigned to such an audit need not have all these attributes, the audit team must collectively possess the requisite attributes, so that it can adequately plan the audit, assess the computer-related controls, test the controls, determine the effect on the overall audit plan, develop findings and recommendations, and report the results. As discussed in the next section of this guide, resources may include be supplemented from outside the organization through partnering or engaging consultants.

Table 1. Knowledge, Skills, and Abilities for IS Security Audit Areas by FISCAM Objective

FISCAM objective	Associated knowledge, skills, and abilities
Organizationwide security program planning and management	Knowledge of the legislative requirements for an agency security program
	Knowledge of the sensitivity of data and the risk management process through risk assessment and risk mitigation
	Knowledge of the risks associated with a deficient security program
	Knowledge of the elements of a good security program
	Ability to analyze and evaluate an organization's security policies and procedures and identify their strengths and weaknesses
Access control	Knowledge across platforms of the access paths into computer systems and of the functions of associated hardware and software providing an access path
	Knowledge of access level privileges granted to users and the technology used to provide and control them
	Knowledge of the procedures, tools, and techniques that provide for good physical, technical, and administrative controls over access
	Knowledge of the risks associated with inadequate access controls
	Ability to analyze and evaluate an organization's access controls and identify the strengths and weaknesses
	Skills to review security software reports and identify access control weaknesses
	Skills to perform penetration testing of the organization's applications and supporting computer systems

[8]*Government Auditing Standards: 1994 Revision* (GAO/OCG-94-4), paragraphs 3.3–3.5, 3.10, and AICPA SAS 94.

[9] FISCAM is a methodology for auditing IS security controls, set forth in the GAO document, *Federal Information Systems Control Audit Manual* (GAO/AIMD-12.19.6, January 1999).

FISCAM objective	Associated knowledge, skills, and abilities
Application software development and change control	Knowledge of the concept of a system life cycle and of the System Development Life Cycle (SDLC) process
	Knowledge of the auditor's role during system development and of federal guidelines for designing controls into systems during development
	Knowledge of the procedures, tools, and techniques that provide control over application software development and modification
	Knowledge of the risks associated with the development and modification of application software
	Ability to analyze and evaluate the organization's methodology and procedures for system development and modification and identify the strengths and weaknesses
System software	Knowledge of the different types of system software and their functions
	Knowledge of the risks associated with system software
	Knowledge of the procedures, tools, and techniques that provide control over the implementation, modification, and use of system software
	Ability to analyze and evaluate an organization's system software controls and identify the strengths and weaknesses
	Skills to use software products to review system software integrity
Segregation of duties	Knowledge of the different functions involved with information systems and data processing and incompatible duties associated with these functions
	Knowledge of the risks associated with inadequate segregation of duties
	Ability to analyze and evaluate an organization's organizational structure and segregation of duties and identify the strengths and weaknesses
Service continuity	Knowledge of the procedures, tools, and techniques that provide for service continuity
	Knowledge of the risks that exist when measures are not taken to provide for service continuity
	Ability to analyze and evaluate an organization's program and plans for service continuity and identify the strengths and weaknesses
Application controls	Knowledge about the practices, procedures, and techniques that provide for the authorization, completeness, and accuracy of application data
	Knowledge of typical applications in each business transaction cycle
	Ability to analyze and evaluate an organization's application controls and identify the strengths and weaknesses
	Skills to use a generalized audit software package to conduct data analyses and tests of application data, and to plan, extract, and evaluate data samples

Auditors performing tasks in two of the above FISCAM areas, access controls (which includes penetration testing) and system software, require additional specialized technical skills. Such technical specialists should have skills in one or more of the categories listed in table 2.

Table 2. KSAs for Information Security Technical Specialists

Specialist	Skills
Network analyst	Advanced knowledge of network hardware and software
	Understanding of data communication protocols
	Ability to evaluate the configuration of routers and firewalls
	Ability to perform external and internal vulnerability tests with manual and automated tools
	Knowledge of the operating systems used by servers

Specialist	Skills
Windows/Novell analyst	Detailed understanding of microcomputer and network architectures
	Ability to evaluate the configuration of servers and the major applications hosted on servers
	Ability to perform internal vulnerability tests with manual and automated tools
Unix analyst	Detailed understanding of the primary variants of the Unix architectures
	Ability to evaluate the configuration of servers and the major applications hosted on servers
	Ability to perform internal vulnerability tests with manual and automated tools
Database analyst	Understanding of the control functions of the major database management systems
	Understanding of the control considerations of the typical application designs that use database systems
	Ability to evaluate the configuration of major database software products
Mainframe system software analyst	Detailed understanding of the design and function of the major components of the operating system
	Ability to develop or modify tools necessary to extract and analyze control information from mainframe computers
	Ability to use audit software tools
	Ability to analyze modifications to system software components
Mainframe access control analyst	Detailed understanding of auditing access control security software such as ACF2, Top Secret, and RACF
	Ability to analyze mainframe audit log data
	Ability to develop or modify tools to extract and analyze access control information

As table 2 shows, some activities require a high degree of IT knowledge, skills, and abilities, while others involve more basic auditing tasks (interviewing, gathering background information, and documenting the IT security environment). Management may therefore want to organize staff with highly specialized technical skills in a separate group with access to special-purpose computer hardware and software. A group of this kind can focus on more technical issues, while other groups within the organization can perform less technical work.

An example of this approach is provided by the New York State Office of the State Comptroller Management Audit Group, which has created a Network Security Facility staffed with in-house IT auditors (part of the Office's Technology Services Unit). The facility, modeled after the successful facility created by the U.S. General Accounting Office, contains an extensive collection of hardware and software that enable staff not only to perform technical audit work, but to continue to develop specialized technical IT skills and expertise. The primary objectives of the facility are to support both financial and performance audits and to provide independent system security audits so that risks are identified and can be addressed in a timely fashion by program managers.

The facility, which is still being developed, is used to simulate and test the computing environments commonly found in New York State agencies. Using the facility's resources, auditors learn in a controlled environment how to use specialized diagnostic software to assess and identify the vulnerabilities in agency controls over information system networks. The auditors also learn how to perform system intrusion tests, in which these vulnerabilities are exploited to gain unauthorized access to the network. (The purpose of this kind of test, which is conducted with the knowledge, cooperation, and participation of agency officials, is to demonstrate the potential consequences of control weaknesses and convince agency officials that the weaknesses need to be addressed.)

Determine How to Fill Skill Gaps

If the assessment of skills reveals gaps, organizations have three options: hiring or training (and retaining) in-house staff, partnering with other organizations, or engaging consultants.

A brief look at each of these possibilities follows.

Using In-House Staff

Hiring. The market for IT and IT security personnel is likely to be highly competitive in the coming years. As noted in an article by Aon Consulting ("Retaining the High-Tech Worker Despite Bottom-Line Uncertainty," *Aon Consulting Forum*, April 2001), "the Information Technology Association of America (ITAA) estimates that 1.6 million high-tech positions were added in 2000. The Bureau of Labor Statistics predicts that demand for computer engineers, computer systems analysts, database administrators, and computer support professionals will more than double by 2006."

It may nonetheless be worthwhile to confront this competition, because the hiring of the right person with the precise capabilities for the job may be exactly what is needed. This is particularly true when experience is a key concern. Experienced IT security professionals will be needed to assess complex networking environments, select the appropriate automated audit tools, and produce key deliverables in the expected timeframe. Paying for experience may be a cost saver in the long run, particularly with respect to advanced technical specialists.

Training Current Personnel. An alternative to hiring is to upgrade the capabilities of current personnel. Depending on the position requirements, this could mean providing additional technical training for audit staff, or it could mean providing audit training to IT staff who already have technical skills.

Table 2, given earlier, presents the knowledge, skills, and abilities (KSAs) established by GAO for information security technical specialists. A review of these requirements may be helpful in determining the training needed to upgrade the capabilities of current staff. One example of the type of curriculum needed is included at appendix E.

Retaining Personnel. Once staff are hired and trained, retaining these highly trained, marketable staff will continue to be a challenge for governments. In planning incentives to retain staff, management would do well to consider the following areas of importance to workers, cited in the Aon Consulting article cited earlier:

Safety and security—Workers respond favorably to organizations that meet or exceed their expectations regarding job security.

Rewards—Workers expect equity both in relation to new hires and to comparable positions in similar organizations.

Affiliation—Employees want to be more than just "workers." They want to be contributors to organizational success.

Growth—High-tech employees want to work for organizations committed to helping them keep pace with the fast-moving technology curve.

Work/life harmony—Employees value an organization that recognizes the importance of the employee's personal and family life.

Offering highly challenging work may be a key factor in retaining staff. In *The Effective Executive* (1966), Peter Drucker observes, "Every survey of young knowledge workers—physicians in the Army Medical Corps, chemists in the research lab, accountants or engineers in the plant, nurses in the hospital—produces the same results. The ones who are enthusiastic and who, in turn, have results to show for their work, are the ones whose abilities are being challenged and used. Those that are deeply frustrated all say, in one way or another: 'My abilities are not being put to use.'"

Partnering

An audit organization could also consider developing a partnership with a local university or other audit organizations on a regional basis to address common security needs. The objective of such partnerships could vary. Possible objectives include sharing staff, sharing information, setting up joint training programs, developing audit approaches, testing software, or sharing complementary personnel and hardware/software resources on a specific audit. The partnership should have a written agreement describing the objectives of the arrangement and the responsibilities of each party, including any compensation for resources and related expense.

Engaging Consultants

Consulting firms offer a variety of services related to information security. For example, specialized services such as penetration testing or network vulnerability testing might be acquired from consultants who could supplement the skills available within an organization. Working with consultants could also be a suitable means of training in-house personnel to perform similar security audit projects. Consultants may offer immediate capabilities not otherwise available without considerable start-up time and cost. Further, consultants could be used to provide services while in-house staff are acquiring more experience and training. These decisions will be based on the relative costs of consulting services and similar in-house capabilities.

Identify and Select Automated Tools

Automated tools—and auditors skilled in their use—are essential in performing an IS security audit to help identify security vulnerabilities. For example:

- Data extraction tools and reporting facilities for access control software can identify users with excess privileges that circumvent segregation of duties.

- Password crackers can identify the use of vendor-default or easily guessed passwords.

- Capture utilities or "sniffers" can identify the transmission of passwords or sensitive information in clear text.

- Scanners, along with standard operating system commands, can help identify an organization's network security profile and determine whether dangerous services are active in components.

- Modem locators can help identify unsecured dial-in modems.

Audit management needs to determine if the organization currently has access to necessary tools and if staff is adequately trained to use them. In addition, some research and analysis will help to determine if other automated tools appropriate for the audit environment should be obtained. The use of automated tools is an area where partnering with other audit organizations may be beneficial. In this way, costs can be shared among several units.

Security software tools are available to develop and monitor security policies, manage access to IT resources, scan networks for vulnerabilities, "crack" encrypted password files, analyze firewall security, detect system intrusions or changes to key system components, and much more.

How might an organization go about selecting the software to meet its needs? Management should consider the factors and questions shown in table 3 when evaluating and selecting security software tools.

Table 3. Key Considerations in Selecting Security Software

Factor	Questions
Value	Of those available, which are critical to provide the services needed by the audit organization?
	Will the tool be valuable to use on in-house systems, agency audits, or both?
	How will the audit team/agency benefit from the use of this tool?
Expertise required	How much specialized knowledge is needed to know when to use the tool?
	How difficult will it be to install and use the tool safely in an active, networked environment?
	What level of experience and expertise is needed to interpret the results provided by the tool?
	Does the complexity of the tool warrant specialized training or expert assistance from an experienced consultant?
	What training is needed to enable auditors to evaluate whether the tools and procedures available will help meet their audit objectives?
Flexibility	Is the tool useful for only certain operating systems such as Unix or Windows NT?
	How much time is needed to deploy the tool and perform the analysis?
Reliability	How old is the tool, and is it currently supported by a reliable technical group?
	How much testing, additional evaluation, and training will be required before the tool can be used? How will the tool be tested and who will do the testing?
	How do tools available as freeware or shareware compare with commercial counterparts?
	Are the sources of freeware and shareware reliable?
Cost	What are the costs and licensing issues involved, including the availability of a traveling license?
Other	What is the expected impact of the software on system or network performance?

These types of questions should be answered when management decides on the services an audit organization will provide and what tools are needed. Audit organizations may want to develop a score sheet weighting the above factors to rate each potential software tool.

Many web sites provide helpful, relevant information to help assess security software tools. Two examples are the CERT Coordination Center (see the security tools listed at *www.cert.org/tech_tips*) and the SANS web site. Further information on those sites and others is given in appendices F and G.

Whether creating or upgrading IS security audit capabilities, organizations should develop a process to select, evaluate, and revise software security tools. The following are recommended steps:

- Research available security tools listing several in each category.

- With your technical partner, IS department, or other state audit agencies, discuss which tools could be most useful in-house and at sites to be audited.

- Determine the degree of platform-specific security software needed.

- Determine a methodology to evaluate and select software.

- Develop a procedure to train personnel in its use.

- Develop a review process to determine whether the software tool has produced results commensurate with its cost.

Developing a methodical approach to selecting and deploying security software tools will provide many benefits:

- Software selected will provide the benefits anticipated both to the audit team and the auditee.

- Time will not be spent on software with limited usefulness or reliability.

- Impact on agency systems will be minimized.

- Training and software costs will be minimized.

- More effective, precise audit recommendations can be made based on specific, relevant data.

- Staff will have the necessary training and experience to implement the software and evaluate the results.

- Auditors will have the knowledge needed to evaluate whether the procedures performed will help meet their audit's objectives.

Proper review and selection of security software tools is crucial in developing a strong IS security audit capability.

Also, the audit organization may wish to partner with other audit organizations or state entities to develop shared facilities or virtual labs.

Assess Costs

When establishing or enhancing IS security audit capabilities, audit management will be faced with various cost considerations that will undoubtedly affect the strategy to achieve the desired capability. (Funding for some costs may not be readily available, and audit management may therefore need to proceed with an interim approach to meeting audit requirements.) Costs can be classified as *human capital* when related to employees of the audit organization, *capital expenditures* when related to the purchase of supporting hardware and software, and *contract dollars* when the capability is procured externally, such as through consultants.

Human capital costs for employees include salaries and benefits that recur anually and generally increase as the cost of living increases. Costs for new employees would include the cost of background checks, particularly important since these employees may eventually have access to critical applications and sensitive information. Both for new employees and for current employees who are new to IS security auditing, training costs can be significant. In addition, significant training costs could be incurred to keep existing auditors up to date with the latest technology, related vulnerabilities, and audit tools. For example, recent catalogs for IS security auditor training showed costs ranging from about $450 to $575 per day per student, although discounts may be available to organizations who register groups or commit to multiple courses.

Because of the breadth of information technology and related tools, an internal IS security audit group would require a number of employees to adequately audit the various environments encountered. For example, one skilled in mainframe technology may not be knowledgeable on network matters. Likewise, one skilled in interviewing and evaluating general controls may not be able to use a generalized audit software package for data sampling, extraction, and analysis. Management must also consider that personnel trained in IS and related technology areas are often more expensive to hire than other auditors.

Capital expenditures are costs to provide IS security auditors the tools to help them do their work, such as computers and licensing fees for audit software. Providing a test facility to support IS auditors with up-to-date hardware and software can require substantial financial resources. For example, one organization expended over $500,000 for hardware and software to establish a test facility, and plans a similar level of expenditures for the next several years to maintain the facility and obtain upgrades of hardware and software entering the market. However, less costly options are possible, such as building a less capable test facility and acquiring hardware and software through nontraditional means. For example, one organization established a test network at a cost of under $2,500, by using existing equipment, surplus computers, and free or near-free software. Here as well, partnering with other organizations may help keep costs lower, where resources of one could be shared with another.

Contract dollars can procure an IS security audit capability through accounting firms and consultants. In recent years, the demand for these services has been high, and as a result contracts could be costly. For example, for a comprehensive review of IS security controls of a large agency, one organization reported that several recent contracted IS security audits had a daily cost that ranged from about $575 to over $630. The time to complete the audits ranged from about 300 to over 1250 days. The actual fees for each audit ranged from over $185,000 to over $725,000. Also, to maintain open competition, as government organizations are required to do, contracting could involve a lengthy process to develop a request for proposals, evaluate the proposals, and select the winning contractor. Accordingly, audit management may choose a strategy that includes a combination of human capital and contract dollars.

Devise Criteria for Project Selection

To protect the credibility and effectiveness of your IS security audit capability, you should develop criteria for project selection. Such criteria might include the following:

- The system should be critical to the stated objective. That is, if the IS security audit is supporting financial statement audits, the audited system should be critical to financial statement accounts or to the financial accounting and reporting process.

- The system should have associated risks, such as confidential data or distributed access (decentralized users).

- The agency owning the system should be cooperative and participate in mitigating the risk of damage during testing.

- The system should be at a manageable level of complexity for the skills and abilities of your information security audit team.

- The audit should fit in the context of the annual and/or long-term audit plan, including adequate and appropriate staff and other resources.

One useful approach is a rotational method of system selection (based on an inventory of key systems). Such a rotation will help ensure that all systems are periodically audited at an appropriate level.

These criteria can be applied in selecting stand-alone projects as well as those projects requesting IS security audit support.

Link Objectives to Supporting Activities

The types of activities required to build or upgrade an IS security audit capability will vary depending on the broader objectives established by the audit organization (see Define Objectives, p 12).

Organizations may want to develop a table such as table 4 (following) to help in determining what activities are needed to satisfy their objectives and who will perform the activities. Using the table, complete each of the following steps:

Establish objectives. Column 1 shows possible IS security audit objectives for a hypothetical audit organization. This column can be tailored to the unique objectives of each state audit organization by adding, deleting, or revising as necessary. (Note: The objectives are repeated on each page of the table.)

Link objectives to supporting activities. For each objective established, the activities required to support that objective can be chosen from those described in columns 2 and 3.

Identify resource gaps. Columns 4 and 5 provide a place for noting who currently provides the activities, and who might perform such activities in the future.

Table 4. Possible IS Security Audit Objectives and Related Activities (Current and Future)

Possible IS security audit objectives (1)	Activities for meeting IS security audit objectives (2)	General description of typical activities (3)	Currently provided by (4)	Provided by in future (5)
Support financial audits Support performance audits Supplement IT audits Provide independent system security audits Support investigative/forensic audits Support CAATs analysis Perform security reviews during system development Support security training program Partner with IS department on security issues	**Planning support**	Determine objectives/scope/timing of support	IS audit	Same
	General controls reviews:		IS audit, financial auditor, performance auditors	Same
	Organization and management	Security responsibilities clearly defined		
	Application development and maintenance	Security over program change controls		
	System software	Operating system security measures in place		
	Computer operations	Sufficient backup, service continuity planning		
	Security administration	Written security plan linked to appropriate procedures		
	Logical security	Security software implementation appropriate		
	Network security	Appropriate security controls		
	Application controls review:		IS audit, financial audit	Same
	Input controls	Security over access rights, passwords		
	Output controls	Security over confidentiality of output files and reports		
	Provide expertise in using automated audit tools, including		Limited	Consultant support, training
	Data extraction and analysis	ACL software	IS audit, financial audit, performance	Same
	Network scanners	ISS, COPS	Proposed	To be determined
	Specialized technical support: Provide expertise in using automated audit tools, including		Proposed	To be determined; review options for joint regional effort with other states/agencies
	Password crackers	Lopht Crack		
	Traffic analyzers (sniffers)	NetXRay		
	Modem locators (war-dialers)	THC-Scan, Tone-LOC		
	Integrity checkers	MD5, Tripwire		
	Intrusion detection/prevention	Snort		

Possible IS security audit objectives (1)	Activities for meeting IS security audit objectives (2)	General description of typical activities (3)	Currently provided by (4)	Provided by in future (5)
Support financial audits Support performance audits Supplement IT audits	**Security information gathering:** Monitor security issues/alerts from external organizations (INFRAGARD, CERT)	Review daily email reports	IS director, IS audit manager	All managers
Provide independent system security audits Support investigative/forensic audits	Monitor legal issues having security implications (e.g., HIPAA—Health Insurance Portability and Accountability Act)	Determine impact, training needed	Various managers	Review options
Support CAATs analysis Perform security reviews during system development	Interface with state CIO, IT directors, and security administrators to address common security issues	Some attendance at joint meetings; no formal mechanism	IS audit manager	Review options with CIO
Support security training program Partner with IS department on security issues	**Other specialized support:** Assist in-house IS department with development and implementation of model security policies, procedures, and controls	Security policy and procedures reviews	IS director	IS director, IS audit
	Assist training department with evaluation, selection, delivery of security training courses	Discuss training needs, options	Training director, consultants	Consultants, in-house instructors
	Develop a test/training network	For use in testing new security software and staff training	Proposed	IS, IS audit

Completing the table may require several iterations. In completing it, organizations should decide first whether the objective requires a new or modified capability.

For organizations establishing an initial IS security audit capability, the table should be helpful in considering a full range of possibilities. These organizations may decide to establish a plan to address high-priority objectives first, adding specific activities as necessary.

Organizations modifying an established IS security audit capability may also use the table to review their current status and determine whether changes are appropriate. For example, reviews of IS general controls have always covered key security issues. However, network security has grown in importance in recent years, raising the question of whether IS audit activities should re-allocate time budgets with greater attention to this area. A review and revision of the table should assist organizations in making such determinations.

Once objectives and related activities are selected, management must determine who will perform those activities and what knowledge, skills, and abilities are needed to do so. Management must also determine whether to build needed resources in-house or acquire them externally (see Assess Skills, p 17).

Use Web-Based Security Research and Training Resources

Resources useful in planning, developing, and sustaining an IS security audit capability are available on many Internet Web sites. While on-line training remains limited, many organizations list information about training courses that are available and offered around the country. Sites offer up-to-date security bulletins and related information about comprehensive training courses, audit and security training, security training for law enforcement, specialized information on certification programs available and related study material, sample audit programs, and generalized information system audit and control information. Below we provide examples of sites by category.

Audit organizations can benefit from this information in many ways:

- Reviewing the information and training available is useful in planning the type of activities and services an audit organization will need to provide.

- These sites provide training departments with a variety of options in developing curricula for their managers and staff.

- Investigative auditors can focus on sites providing training information for cybercrime.

- The IS/IT department can review sites to stay current on the latest vulnerabilities discovered and fixes available.

General IS Audit Information

www.isaca.org—ISACA provides information on generally applicable and accepted standards for good information technology security and control practices. The site also provides a global information repository to help members keep pace with technological change.

www.itaudit.org and *www.auditnet.org*—these two key sites provide sample audit programs, checklists, articles, tools, and other resources developed for the benefit of the audit profession.

IT and IT Security Training and Information

www.sans.org—The System Administration, Networking, and Security (SANS) Institute provides security updates, research and publications, training courses, and certification on a wide range of IT security topics.

www.cert.org—Formerly known as the Computer Emergency Response Team, the CERT® Coordination Center (CERT/CC) is a center of Internet security expertise. It is located at the Software Engineering Institute, a federally funded research and development center operated by Carnegie-Mellon University.

www.misti.com—The MIS Training Institute provides audit and security training worldwide. Its divisions provide information security conferences, seminars, and consulting services, including hands-on audit and security training.

www.brainbuzz.com—This site provides training and study guides for hundreds of certification programs for products from vendors such as Cisco, Microsoft, Novell, Lotus, IBM, Sun, CITRIX, Oracle, and many more.

Data Extraction and Analysis Tools

www.acl.com—ACL Services Ltd. is a privately held company based in Vancouver, Canada, with offices in Brussels and Singapore and representatives worldwide. Since 1987, ACL has offered an integrated solution for auditors, including software, training and consulting services, a worldwide support network, and industry-focused publications.

www.audimation.com/index.htm—Audimation Services Inc. (ASI) was formed in 1992 to distribute IDEA (Interactive Data Extraction & Analysis) software to audit departments in industry and government. IDEA is a PC-based file interrogation package that allows accountants, auditors, and financial managers to view, extract, sample, analyze and test data from any other system. Originally developed by the Canadian Institute of Chartered

Accountants, IDEA was acquired by CaseWare International Inc., which founded CaseWare-IDEA Inc. to further develop the software.

www.audittools.com—AuditTools is a privately held company based in Oslo, Norway, that markets IDEA (see above).

Cybercrime

www.nctp.org—The National Cybercrime Training Partnership (NCTP) provides training to law enforcement on high-technology crime.

Further information on these and other Web sites is provided in appendices F and G.

III. Measuring and Monitoring the IS Audit Capability

Purpose of measuring and monitoring results

Monitoring the information system security audit process

Monitoring key performance indicators

Assessing performance of critical success factors
Devising key performance measures

Performing evaluations
Assessing auditee satisfaction
Issuing progress reports

Establishing or identifying benchmarks for the information system security audit capability

Independence
Professional ethics and standards
Competence and retention of qualified staff
Planning

Using performance and reporting measures

Performance measures of audit work
Reporting measures
Measures for follow-up activities

The graphic above provides an overview of the contents on this section. The boxes should not be interpreted as sequential steps, but as indications of the topics covered.

Purpose of Measuring and Monitoring Results

Organizations measure and monitor results in order to assess performance. Effective performance measurement and monitoring requires each audit organization to clearly define its IS security audit mission and objectives (section II). It further requires that the audit organization establish both long-term strategic goals (three to five years) and short-term (less than three years) goals. Each audit organization should measure its performance against previously established goals and report on related progress.

The goals of the IS security audit capability should flow from its mission statement. The following are examples of such goals:

- Audit and evaluation results and recommendations are effective.

- Audits and evaluations meet professional standards and legal requirements.

- The IS security audit capability will attract and retain highly qualified, motivated, and dedicated individuals.

- The work environment will foster and value trust, open communication, and professional enrichment.

Each audit organization needs to set the agenda for its IS security audit capability according to its own environment, needs, and abilities. Although each audit organization will differ in its approach to IS security auditing, all organizations should seek to become results-oriented by performing the following key steps:

- monitoring the information system security audit process and

- assessing the information system security audit capability.

Monitoring the Information System Security Audit Process

Monitoring Key Performance Indicators

For the IS security audit process, management should ensure that relevant performance indicators (e.g., benchmarks) from both internal and external sources are defined. Management should determine performance benchmarks for each area to be measured and then develop statistics that compare the benchmarks to actual practice. For example, a benchmark regarding competency might be that the IS department should have at least 65 percent of its auditors with Certified Information Systems Auditor (CISA) designations or with graduate degrees in computer science or management information systems.

Assessing Performance of Critical Success Factors

Services to be delivered by the IS security audit capability should be measured and compared with target levels. This requires the identification of key performance measures and/or critical success factors. Assessments of the IS security audit capability should be performed on an ongoing basis.

To achieve strategic and short-term goals, management should use past performance information to determine priorities for current and future projects. Using a number of these performance measures and performing regular evaluations are necessary to judge progress towards the goals and objectives.

Devising Key Performance Measures

The achievement of strategic goals and objectives can be demonstrated through both quantitative and qualitative performance goals and measures. Collectively, these performance goals and measures will, along with actual results, enable an organization to evaluate the timeliness and quality of service provided by the IS security audit capability. Measuring performance also helps bring about improvements in operations and accountability appropriate for a results-oriented style of government. For the defined strategic goals and objectives, the following measures of results could be used:

- financial benefits, as measured by savings and efficiencies identified by the audit work and acted upon by the auditee;

- improvements in IS security to which the audit work contributed; and

- recommendations made, and subsequently implemented, to correct underlying causes of problems that impede IS security awareness, efficiency, and effectiveness.

For each of the strategic objectives, organizations should use qualitative, multiyear performance goals intended to capture the breadth and depth of the work performed by the IS security capability.

Performing Evaluations

To help assess actual progress against the strategic objectives, periodic evaluations should be used. One of the most important of these is the evaluation of actions taken by auditees in response to the IS security audit recommendations. Each IS security audit capability should actively monitor the status of open recommendations, report on them at least annually, and use the results of the analysis of this monitoring to determine the need for further work in a particular area. For example, if an auditee has not undertaken a recommended action that is still considered valid and worthwhile, a decision may be made to pursue further action with governmental officials or undertake additional work.

In addition, each IS security audit capability should conduct evaluations to improve the timeliness and quality of the audit work. Samples of completed assignments should be reviewed to determine their adherence to auditing and other quality assurance standards, and the results of this review should be used to correct any identified weaknesses.

Each IS security audit capability should evaluate its administration, including key performance measurements. Such evaluations are useful for ensuring that operations are efficient and economical.

Periodic peer reviews should be used to provide an independent assessment of quality controls.

Assessing Auditee Satisfaction

At regular intervals, the audit organization should measure the satisfaction of auditees with the services delivered by the IS security audit capability, to identify shortfalls in service levels and establish improvement objectives. Accordingly, the IS security audit capability should establish an auditee satisfaction survey designed to measure the following:

- professionalism of IS audit staff in both demeanor and appearance;

- technical understanding of areas reviewed;

- ability to communicate effectively (both verbally and in writing) with auditee personnel;

- effective use of time and agency resources;

- ability to maintain a positive and productive relationship with auditee personnel; and

- professionalism in reporting findings to entities other than the auditee, including reporting the findings in such a manner that the weaknesses identified by the auditor could not be readily used by unauthorized parties (i.e., hackers) to attack the agency.

Issuing Progress Reports

Progress reports should be provided for management's review of the organization's progress toward identified goals. Upon review of these progress reports, appropriate management action should be initiated.

Establishing or Identifying Benchmarks for the Information System Security Audit Capability

Independence

It is generally understood that the IS security audit capability should be independent of the area being audited so that the audit will be objective. However, to help ensure that this independence exists both in fact and perception, it is recommended that an independence and outside employment policy be used. Each member of the IS security audit staff should be required to annually complete and sign an independence questionnaire that refers to this policy.

Professional Ethics and Standards

The IS security audit capability should ensure adherence to applicable codes of professional ethics (e.g., Code of Professional Ethics of the Information Systems Audit and Control Association) and auditing standards (e.g., *Government Auditing Standards*) in all that they do. Due professional care should be exercised in all aspects of the audit work, including the observance of applicable audit and information technology standards. Audit criteria should be used where applicable and adherence to the *Federal Information System Control Audit Manual* (FISCAM) should be considered.

For measurement of compliance with auditing standards, several possibilities exist. If an audit organization having an IS security audit capability undergoes regular peer reviews, it would be appropriate to ensure that during these overall reviews, at least one IS audit is included in each review, so that compliance with the appropriate auditing standards can be assessed. In addition, internal reviews of selected IS audits should be performed to ensure adherence to standards and specified criteria. These internal reviews should be part of a formal program with specific guidance on reporting the results of the reviews and follow-up and corrective action plans.

Competence and Retention of Qualified Staff

Benchmarks in this area might include that a specific percentage of IS security staff possess professional certifications and/or have graduate degrees in specified disciplines. For example, a benchmark could be that 65 percent of IS security staff be a CISA or have a graduate degree in computer science or management information systems. In addition, there should be benchmarks with respect to the amount and nature of continuing professional education that each IS auditor must obtain annually. For example, a benchmark could be that each IS auditor is required to obtain at least 20 hours of continuing professional education in IS-related subjects or managerial subjects each year and 120 hours over a three-year period.

Planning

A plan should be established to ensure that regular and independent IS security audits are obtained for all critical information systems and applications. To measure the applicability and appropriateness of such a plan, there must be a central repository of information regarding each auditee, its critical applications, and their scope, function, and nature. The measurement function should assess the completeness and accuracy of the central repository of auditees' information systems and applications by selecting various agencies and verifying information on a test basis.

Using Performance and Reporting Measures

Performance Measures of Audit Work

Audits should be appropriately supervised to provide assurances that audit objectives are achieved and applicable professional auditing standards are met. Auditors should ensure that they obtain sufficient, reliable, relevant, and useful evidence to achieve the audit objectives. The audit findings and conclusions are to be supported by appropriate analysis and interpretation of this evidence. Determinations should be made as to whether the work was performed in accordance with the predetermined budgeted amount of time and if the work was completed by established deadlines. Relevant objectives and associated measurements for this could be as follows:

Objective: Actual audit time does not exceed budgeted time by more than 10 percent for all completed assignments.

Measurement: Accumulate all actual times and compare to budgets to determine cumulative over/underrun for all completed audits.

Objective: Fieldwork for 90 percent of all audits must be completed within a given timeframe (e.g., 6 months).

Measurement: Determine percentage of audits completed within the specified timeframe (based on reports issued).

Reporting Measures

The organization's audit function should provide a report, in an appropriate form, to intended recipients upon the completion of audit work. The audit report should state the scope and objectives of the audit, the period of coverage, the nature and extent of the audit work performed, and the associated audit standards. The report should identify the organization, the intended recipients, and any restrictions on circulation. The audit report should also state the findings, conclusions, and recommendations concerning the audit work performed and any reservations or qualifications that the auditor has with respect to the audit. There should be a determination made that the audit report does not disclose exception conditions in such a manner that outside parties could exploit the information and compromise the auditees' networks. Finally, the reports should be issued in a timely manner, so that they may be useful to agency management and other interested parties.

Specifically, a metric should be established such as the following:

Objective: 80 percent of draft reports should be issued within 90 days from the completion of fieldwork.

Measurement: Determine percentage of reports issued within the targeted timeframe (e.g., measured from fieldwork completion to the date of the issuance of the related audit report).

Measures for Follow-up Activities

Resolution of audit comments rests with the management of the auditee. There should be established procedures for determining whether auditee management has taken appropriate action in a timely manner on previous findings and recommendations. Performance measures should be established to determine whether the auditees have agreed with the findings of the auditors for a specified percentage of the audit findings and whether they have implemented a specified percentage of the audit findings within a given time period. Specifically, the following objectives and related measurements could be implemented:

Objective: 90 percent of report recommendations are accepted by agency management.

Measurement: Determine percentage of report recommendations accepted in the formal response by agency management measured over a specified time period.

Objective: 60 percent of report recommendations are implemented by the auditees over a specified period (i.e., within the audit cycle or other designated period).

Measurement: Determine percentage of report recommendations implemented during the specified period.

Appendix A.

Auditing Standards Placing New Emphasis on IT Controls

Below are examples of recently revised auditing standards that place a stronger emphasis on assessing the risk associated with information technology and evaluating relevant IT controls, including controls over information security.

SAS No. 94

The AICPA's Statement on Auditing Standards (SAS) No. 94, effective for audits of financial statements for periods beginning on or after June 1, 2001, amended SAS No. 55 and provides guidance to auditors about the effect of information technology on internal control, and on the auditor's understanding of internal control and assessment of control risk. The statement is titled *The Effect of Information Technology on the Auditor's Consideration of Internal Control in a Financial Statement Audit.* The Auditing Standards Board (ASB) believes the guidance is needed because entities of all sizes increasingly are using IT in ways that affect their internal control and the auditor's consideration of internal control in a financial statement audit. Consequently, in some circumstances, auditors may need to perform tests of controls to perform an effective audit. Essentially SAS 94 recognizes that a purely substantive testing methodology accompanied by the prerequisite documentation of the auditors' understanding of the system may *not* be sufficient regardless of control risk assessment, i.e., assessing control risk at the maximum.

Amendment No. 1, *Government Auditing Standards* (Yellow Book)

In May 1999, the GAO issued Amendment No. 1, entitled "Documentation Requirements When Assessing Control Risk at Maximum for Controls Significantly Dependent Upon Computerized Information Systems." The effect of the amendment was to add to *Government Auditing Standards* a documentation requirement for those entities that utilize information systems. If, in a Yellow Book financial statement audit, the entity is significantly dependent upon computerized information systems, the auditor must provide specific information in the working papers when the decision is made to assess control risk at the maximum. The auditor is required to address either the ineffectiveness of the design and operation of the computer controls or the reasons why it would be ineffective to test the controls. The reason for the requirement is to ensure that the auditor documents whether the decision was made as a matter of audit efficiency or because there were perceived weaknesses in computer controls. GAO believes that the documentation requirement will focus the auditor's attention on the nature of computer controls and whether some benefit might be obtained by a test of those controls.

SAS No. 80

The ASB's SAS No. 80, effective for engagements beginning on or after January 1, 1997, amended SAS No. 31 and recognized the rapid migration of evidence to electronic format. The statement observed that "Because of the growth in the use of computers and other information technology, many entities process significant information electronically. Accordingly, it may be difficult or impossible for the auditor to access certain information for inspection, inquiry, or confirmation without using information technology." In addition, SAS No. 80 stated, "In entities where significant information is transmitted, processed, maintained, or accessed electronically, the auditor may determine that it is not practical or possible to reduce detection risk to an acceptable level by performing only substantive tests for one or more financial statement assertions."

Appendix B.

Federal Legislation, Rules, and Directives Applicable to Information Security Since 1974

Below are brief descriptions of the federal legislation, rules, and directives that have impacted information security since 1974.

Privacy Act of 1974—requires agencies to inform the public of the existence of a system of records containing personal information, to give individuals access to records about themselves, and to manage those records in a way that ensures fairness to individuals in agency programs.

Counterfeit Access Device and Computer Fraud and Abuse Act of 1984—makes it a criminal offense to knowingly access a computer without authorization or to obtain certain classified information or certain financial records covered under the Privacy Act of 1978.

Computer Fraud and Abuse Act of 1986—extended the information coverage of the Counterfeit Access Device and Computer Fraud and Abuse Act of 1984 to include medical records, examinations, diagnoses, care, and treatment. It also made unauthorized use of passwords a criminal offense.

Electronic Communications Privacy Act of 1986—broadens the definitions of electronic communications to include computers for prosecution of unauthorized interception of communications. It also allows for recovery of civil damages as well as criminal penalties.

Computer Security Act of 1987, as amended by the Information Technology Act of 1996 (there is also an amendment being considered in 2001)—directs the National Institute of Standards and Technology to establish a computer standards program for federal computer systems, including security of such systems. It also requires federal agencies to implement computer security programs.

Paperwork Reduction Act of 1995—minimizes the paperwork burden for individuals, small businesses, educational and nonprofit institutions, federal contractors, state, local, and tribal governments, and other persons resulting from the collection of information by or for the federal government. It requires compliance with Computer Security Act of 1987.

Health Insurance Portability and Accountability Act of 1996 (HIPAA)—enacted primarily as a way to allow individuals to carry health insurance from employer to employer, but includes provisions for the United States Department of Health and Human Services to develop electronic data interchange, privacy, and information security standards. Although the electronic data interchange and privacy standards were primarily developed to enable the efficient electronic transmission of certain health information, the proposed information security standard is applicable to any personally identifiable health information that is electronically maintained or transmitted. HIPAA also provides for civil and criminal penalties for noncompliance, including fines up to $25,000 for multiple violations of the same requirement, and fines up to $250,000, imprisonment up to 10 years, or both, for the wrongful disclosure of individually identifiable health information with the intent to sell that information.

Uniform Computer Information Transactions Act (UCITA) of 1999—provides a uniform commercial code for software licenses and other computer information transactions that focuses on contracts involving computer information, including electronic contracts. To date, very few states have adopted the UCITA.

Uniform Electronic Transaction Act (UETA) of 1999—provides a uniform commercial code that recognizes the equivalence of electronic records and writings and the validity of electronic signatures to authorize transactions. To date, most states have adopted UETA or similar legislation or are considering it.

Electronic Signatures in Global and National Commerce Act (2000)—allows electronic signatures to have the same legal authority as written signatures to authorize transactions.

Presidential Decision Directive—63 (1998), "Critical Infrastructure Protection"—directs agencies to take appropriate actions to protect the nation's critical infrastructures from intentional acts that would diminish national security missions, general public health and safety, and government's ability to deliver essential public services, and to ensure orderly functioning of the economy.

Office of Management and Budget (OMB) Circular A-130, "Management of Federal Information Resources"—establishes policy for the management of federal information resources, incorporating the Paperwork Reduction Act.

OMB Circular A-133, "Audits of State, Local Governments, and Non-Profit Organizations"—requires that organizations receiving a defined level of federal funding obtain financial audits that follow generally accepted governmental auditing standards.

Assessing the IS Infrastructure

1. Check all operating systems that are present in your government's organization.

System	Approximate number
OS/390	
UNIX	
AIX	
HP-UX	
LINUX	
SUN	
Novell	
NT	
UNISYS	
Other (specify):	

2. Check all networking components that are present in your government's organization:

System	Approximate number
VTAM/JES	
CICS	
Routers	
Firewalls	
Protocols	
EDI/E-commerce	
Encryption	
Digital signatures	

3. Check all environmental security products that are present in your government's organization:

System	Approximate number
ACF2	
RACF	
Top Secret	
UNICENTER	
AXENT	
Other (specify):	

_____

_____

4. Check all database management systems that are used in your government's organization.

System	Approximate number
Oracle	
DB2	
IDMS	

5. Check all the tools that your office has licenses for and specify specific tools when applicable. (Examples are listed in parentheses.)

System	Approximate number
CA-Examine	
Port scanners (nmap)	
Network test scanners (CyberCop Scanner, Internet Security Scanner)	
Tone locator (THC-SCAN)	
Crackers (L0phtCrack, John the Ripper)	
Sniffers (NetXRay)	
DumpACL	
DYL	
SAS	
IDEA	

Skills Self-Assessment for Information Security Audit Function Personnel

Employee Name:

Ability to assess/evaluate an entity's:	Self-assessment of capability/interest in control area				Training desired	
	Expert	Proficient	Capable	Strong interest	**Yes**	**No**
Entitywide Security Program Planning and Management						
Compliance with legislative and other requirements for an agency security program						
Computer security risk assessment						
Computer security program plan and related policies and procedures						
Awareness of its computer security risks and responsibilities						
Monitoring of its computer security program's effectiveness						
Access Control						
Risk classification of entity systems and data						
Process for authorizing system users and granting system access						
Physical security over its computer systems						
Logical security over its computer systems: (see technical areas below and tools later)						
Operating systems: OS/390						
UNIX: AIX						
HP-UX						
LINUX						
SUN						
NOVELL						
NT						
UNISYS						
Other AS/400 (OS/400)						
Networking: VTAM/JES						
CICS						
Routers						
Firewalls						
Protocols						
EDI/E-Commerce						
Encryption						
Digital Signatures						
Environmental security products: ACF2						
RACF						
Top Secret						
UNICENTER						
AXENT						

Ability to assess/evaluate an entity's:		Self-assessment of capability/interest in control area				Training desired	
		Expert	Proficient	Capable	Strong interest	Yes	No
	Other (specify)						
Database management systems:	Oracle						
	DB2						
	IDMS						
Monitoring of system access							
Application Software Development and Change Control							
Use of software tools in its life cycle management (e.g., CA-Endevor)							
SDLC policies and procedures							
Control over application software libraries							
System Software (see technical areas above and tools below)							
Installation and configuration of system software							
Access control to system software							
Monitoring of system software use							
System software configuration management							
Segregation of Duties							
Organizational structure and segregation of duties and identify the strengths and weaknesses							
Service Continuity							
Contingency plan							
Contingency plan testing							
Application Controls (see also related tools below)							
Effectiveness of the design of the application's authorization, completeness, and accuracy controls							
CAATs							
Analyze data files							
Tools (used in our assessment/evaluation of entity)							
	CA-Examine						
	Port scanners: nmap						
	Network test scanners: CyberCop Scanner Internet Security Scanner						
	Tone locator: THC-Scan						
	Crackers (L0phtCrack, John the Ripper)						
	Sniffers (NetXRay)						
	DumpACL						
	DYL						
	SAS						
	IDEA						
	Scripts (PERL, REXX)						
Forensics							
Analyze storage devices for electronic evidence recovery							

Ability to assess/evaluate an entity's:	Self-assessment of capability/interest in control area				Training desired	
	Expert	Proficient	Capable	Strong interest	Yes	No
Tools						
Data mining software (specify)						
Data recovery software (specify)						
Disk cleansing software (specify)						
Other Tools						
Office Suite products						
Standard OS commands & utilities						
Data analysis						
Sampling						
Integrated test facility						
Other (Specify) CGI/JAVA/ACTIVEX Computer Forensics						

Education and Professional Certifications

Degree	University/College
1.	
2.	
3.	
Professional Certifications	
1. CPA:	
2. CISA:	
3. CGFM:	
4. CIA:	
5. CCP:	
6. CFE:	

Definitions

Self-Assessment (Select one category)

Expert: Have extensive experience; could instruct others on subject matter or give guidance on performance of audit tasks

Proficient: Could perform audit tasks with no start-up time needed to research area or acquire skills

Capable: Believe could perform audit tasks but may require some supervision and/or start-up time to research area or acquire skills

Strong interest: Have a strong interest in working or acquiring skills in area

IT Security Curriculum

Level I. Foundation Courses

All staff (with advanced reading required and pre-testing; waivers for equivalent)

IS audit methodology overview (FISCAM)
TCP/IP—Introduction
Networking—Introduction
Network security—Introduction
Firewalls and perimeter security—Introduction
Web security—Introduction
IS audit methodology areas
- General controls
  Entitywide security management
  Logical access controls/segregation
  Physical and environmental controls
  System software
  Configuration management/change control
  Service continuity
- Application controls

Understanding and meeting SAS 94 requirements
Interpreting and understanding SAS 70 reports

Level II. General Network Operating Systems

Recommended for all staff (with introductory course or equivalent experience requirement)

Windows
UNIX

Level III. Specialized Skills

Recommended for selected staff.

Mainframe security software and operating systems
- OS/390
- CA-ACF2
- CA-Top Secret
- RACF
- CA-EXAMINE

Database
- SQL
- Oracle
- DB2

Advanced networking
- Firewalls
- Routers/switches

Intrusion detection

Forensic analysis

CAATs

Testing/analysis tool operation to perform vulnerability assessments

PKI and encryption

EDI

Level IV. Advanced Technical Skills

Individually tailored curriculum

Appendix F.
Training Information: Internet Sites

http://www.sans.org

The SANS (System Administration, Networking, and Security) Institute is a cooperative research and education organization through which more than 96,000 system administrators, security professionals, and network administrators share the lessons they are learning and find solutions to the challenges they face. SANS was founded in 1989.

The core of the institute is the many security practitioners in government agencies, corporations, and universities around the world who invest hundreds of hours each year in research and teaching to help the entire SANS community. During 2000 and 2001, this core will grow rapidly as the Global Incident Analysis Center (GIAC) and the GIAC Certification programs develop mentors who will help new security practitioners master the basics.

The SANS community creates four types of products:

- System and security alerts and news updates
- Special research projects and publications
- In-depth education
- Certification

Many SANS resources, such as news digests, research summaries, security alerts, and award-winning papers are free to all who ask. Income from printed publications funds university-based research programs. The GIAC and special research projects are funded by income from SANS educational programs.

http://www.cert.org

The CERT® Coordination Center (CERT/CC) is a center of Internet security expertise. It is located at the Software Engineering Institute, a federally funded research and development center operated by Carnegie-Mellon University.

The CERT/CC studies Internet security vulnerabilities, handles computer security incidents, publishes a variety of security alerts, does research for long-term changes in networked systems, and develops information and training to help improve security.

http://www.misti.com/

Founded in 1978, the MIS Training Institute reports that it is the international leader in audit and information security training, with offices in the USA, UK, and Asia. The MIS's security and consulting division, the Information Security Institute (ISI), focuses exclusively on providing high-quality information security conferences, seminars, and consulting services. System Security Ltd., a UK division of MIS, provides hands-on audit and security training.

http://www.gocsi.com

The Computer Security Institute (CSI) reports that it is the world's leading membership organization specifically dedicated to serving and training the information, computer, and network security professional.

Since 1974, CSI has been providing education and aggressively advocating the critical importance of protecting information assets.

CSI sponsors two conference and exhibitions each year (NetSec in June and the CSI Annual in November) and seminars on encryption, intrusion management, Internet, firewalls, awareness, Windows, and more.

CSI membership benefits include the ALERT newsletter, a quarterly journal, and a buyers guide. CSI also publishes surveys and reports on topics such as computer crime and information security program assessment; it also disseminates an electronic Information Protection Assessment Kit (IPAK).

http://www.nctp.org

The stated vision of the National Cybercrime Training Partnership (NCTP) is to develop a 21st century paradigm for law enforcement training in electronic and high-technology crime. This newly designed training paradigm must feature multilevel, multitiered, decentralized, and continuous training. This training will be

- available to multiple types of law enforcement personnel (e.g., investigators, prosecutors, and specialists);

- decentralized to reach law enforcement personnel in all geographic regions and all levels of government; and

- continuous to remain current with the rapidly changing technology and associated threat.

The NCTP stated mission is to provide guidance and assistance to local, state, and federal law enforcement agencies in an effort to ensure that the law enforcement community is properly trained to address electronic and high-technology crime.

Appendix G.
Additional Web Resources

www.acl.com

www.atstake.com/index.html

www.auditnet.org

www.canaudit.com

www.ciac.org/ciac/

www.cs.purdue.edu/coast

www.cyberarmy.com

www.isaca.org

www.itaudit.org

www.rootshell.com

www.sandstorm.com

www.securityfocus.com

www.securitysearch.net

www.sso.org/nasact/

www.technotronic.com/

www.unix-wizards.com